English Code 6

Phonics Book

International Phonetic Alphabet (IPA)

IPA SYMBOLS

Consonants

/b/	bag, bike
/d/	desk, opened
/f/	face, free, laugh, photo
/g/	game, good
/h/	hit, hot
/k/	key, kite
/l/	lamp, lucky
/m/	man, monkey
/n/	neck, nut
/ŋ/	ring, flying
/p/	pen, pink
/r/	run, rock
/s/	sun, sell, cycle, grapes
/ʃ/	shirt, shut, shell
/t/	tent, knocked
/θ/	thick, thirsty
/ð/	this, there
/v/	visit, give
/w/	wall, window, what
/ks/	relax, taxi
/j/	yellow, young
/z/	zoo, bananas
/tʃ/	chair, cheese, cheap
/dʒ/	jeans, juice, judge, ginger

Two-Letter Consonant Blend

/bl/	blanket, blue
/pl/	plane, planet
/kl/	clean, climb
/gl/	glass, glove
/fl/	fly, floor
/sl/	sleep, slow
/br/	break, branch
/pr/	price, practice
/kr/	crab
/fr/	fruit
/gr/	grass
/dr/	draw
/tr/	train
/ŋk/	bank, think
/nd/	stand, round
/nt/	student, count
/sk/	scarf, skirt, basket, scary
/sm/	small
/sn/	snow
/sp/	sports, space
/st/	stand, first, stay
/sw/	swim, sweet
/tw/	twelve, twins
/kw/	quick, question

Three-Letter Consonant Blend

/spr/	spring
/str/	street
/skr/	screen
/skw/	square

Vowels

🇺🇸 /ɑː/ 🇬🇧 /ɒ/	top, jog, wash
/æ/	cat, clap, sand
/e/	wet, send, healthy
/ɪ/	hit, sing, pin
/ɔː/	caught, saw, cough
🇺🇸 /ɔːr/ 🇬🇧 /ɔː/	horse, morning
/eɪ/	cake, name, say
/iː/	eat, tree, steam
🇺🇸 /oʊ/ 🇬🇧 /əʊ/	home, coat, snow
/uː/	food, glue, flew, June
/ʌ/	duck, run, cut, honey
/ʊ/	cook, foot, put
🇺🇸 /ər/ 🇬🇧 /ə/	ruler, teacher
/ɜːr/	bird, hurt, word, learn

Diphthongs

/aɪ/	nice, bike
/aʊ/	house, brown
/ɔɪ/	boil, enjoy
🇺🇸 /ɑːr/ 🇬🇧 /aː/	card, market
🇺🇸 /aɪr/ 🇬🇧 /aɪə/	fire, hire
🇺🇸 /aʊr/, /aʊər/ 🇬🇧 /aʊər/	hour, flower
🇺🇸 /er/ 🇬🇧 /eə/	chair, bear, there
🇺🇸 /ɪr/ 🇬🇧 /ɪə/	near, engineer
/juː/	cute, huge, few

Vowel and Consonant Blend

/ʃən/	station, dictionary
/ɪz/	beaches, bridges
/ɪd/	visited

Contents

1 a / o

1 Listen, point, and repeat.

a

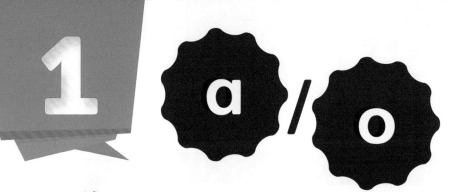

1

w**a**sh

3

wh**a**t

5

w**a**nt

o

2

f**o**g

4

h**o**t

6

sh**o**p

🇺🇸 American	🇬🇧 British
favorite	favourite

I want to shop, shop, shop.
It's my favorite thing.
What was it I wanted?
Almost everything!
I feel sorry
When I have to stop.
I want to shop, shop, shop.
It's my favorite thing.

I want to ...

3 💡 💬 **What do you want to do?**
Sing the song again with another verb.

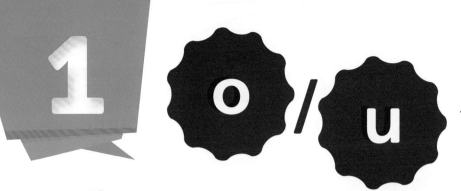

1 o/u

4 🎧 05 Listen, point, and repeat.

o

u

1 son

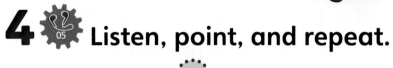

2 brush

3 honey

4 hug

5 money

6 hungry

5  Listen. Then say.

🇺🇸 American	🇬🇧 British
three thirty	half past three

My brother is eating dim sum
And he wants me to have some.
But I want some chicken curry,
I can't wait for it to come!
Our mother isn't hungry,
So she just has a cup of tea.
Together we have so much fun
Until it's half past three.

6  What's your favorite food? Tell a partner.

1 u / oo

7 🎧 Listen, point, and repeat.

u

oo

1

p**u**t

2

b**oo**k

3

p**u**sh

4

c**oo**k

5

c**u**shion

6

g**oo**d

8  Listen and read.

My cat likes to read books. She puts the book on the table. She carefully turns the pages.

Then she pushes the book back onto the shelf. What a good cat!

9 Write another story about a friend.

2

1 🎧 Listen, point, and repeat.

short

1

headline

2

healthy

3

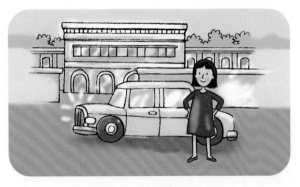

wealthy

long

4

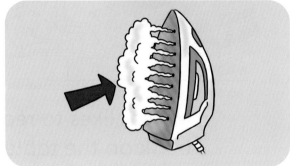

steam

5

eat

6

sea

2  Listen. Then sing.

* I wish you health,
I wish you wealth,
I wish you happiness.
May all of your dreams come true.

You may travel across the sea,
But you know you'll always be
A very special friend to me.

* Repeat

3 Write a card to a special friend.

I wish you ...

Review 1

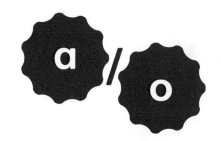

1 🔊 12 💬 **Listen and say the words. Then find the words in the grid.**

a

cat   wash

o

shop   honey

u

drum   push

oo

cook   food

ea

head   sea

h	b	w	a	s	h	c	s
o	g	i	z	n	p	d	h
n	f	p	u	s	h	u	o
e	o	w	y	v	e	m	p
y	o	q	z	h	a	c	l
c	d	c	o	o	d	a	k
h	j	o	e	g	h	t	m
e	f	o	f	s	e	a	t
z	u	k	i	d	r	u	m

3

oa / ow

1 Listen, point, and repeat.

oa

ow

1

boat

2

blow

3

coat

4

flow

5

road

6

snow

2 🎧 💬 Listen. Then say.

The wind may blow,
It may rain or snow,
But I know where I want to be.

In a long red coat,
On my nice little boat,
Going slowly out to sea.

3 💡 💬 Where do you want to be when you grow up?

3 ew/ue

4 Listen, point, and repeat.

ew

1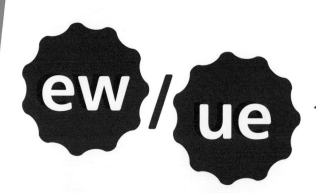

view

2

few

3

interview

ue

4

Sue

5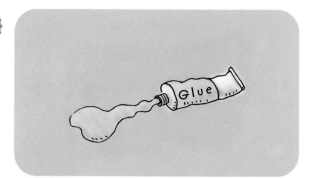

glue

6

clue

5 Listen. Then say.

This morning at half past three,
Sue woke up very suddenly.
Today was her interview,
And there was nothing much to do.
For there are only very few,
Who wake up early and see the view.

6 What can you see when you wake up early?
Tell a partner.

4

au / aw / ou

1 🎧17 Listen, point, and repeat.

1

caught

2

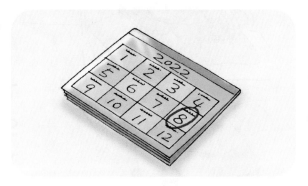

August

3

saw

4

claws

5

bought

6

thought

2  **Listen and read.**

🇺🇸 American	🇬🇧 British
smart	clever

I always go fishing in August.

I caught two crabs in the sea.

I taught the crabs how to sing and dance.

They waved their claws so happily.

I never saw such clever crabs.

They should be on TV!

3  **Write a funny story about you and an animal. Read it to the class.**

4

ue / ew / u_e

4 🎧 19 **Listen, point, and repeat.**

1

bl**ue**

2

		T	F
1	The sun rises in the East.	✓	☐

tr**ue**

3

dr**ew**

4

fl**ew**

5

J**u**n**e**

6

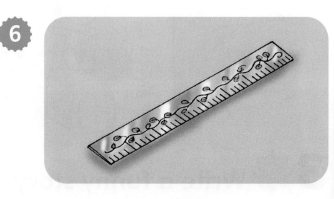

r**u**l**er**

5  Listen. Then say.

In June I drew a picture of a flower.
It grew and grew and grew.
Soon there were blue flowers everywhere.
Do you believe it's true?

In June I drew a picture of a bird.
And off the page it flew.
Soon there were blue birds everywhere.
Do you believe it's true?

6 Draw your own picture. Show it to a partner.

I drew a picture of …

19

Review 2

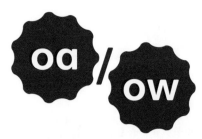

1 🎧 **21** Play the game. Listen and say the words.
Then say words with the same sound.

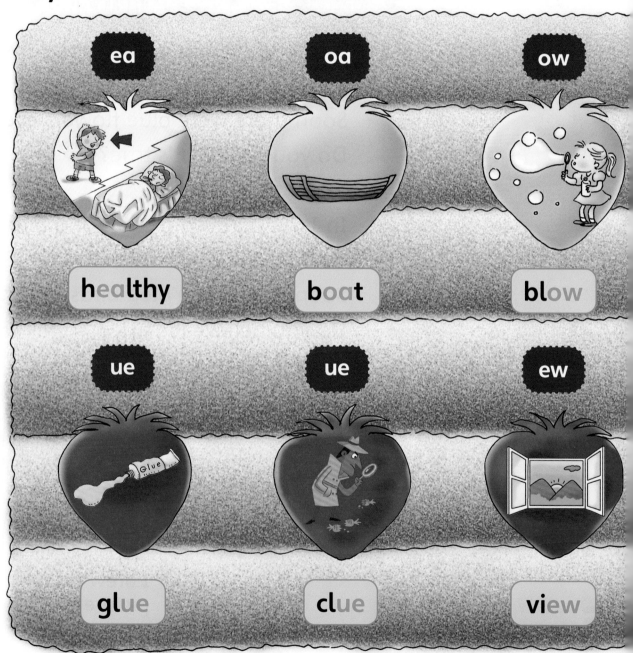

ea	oa	ow
healthy	boat	blow

ue	ue	ew
glue	clue	view

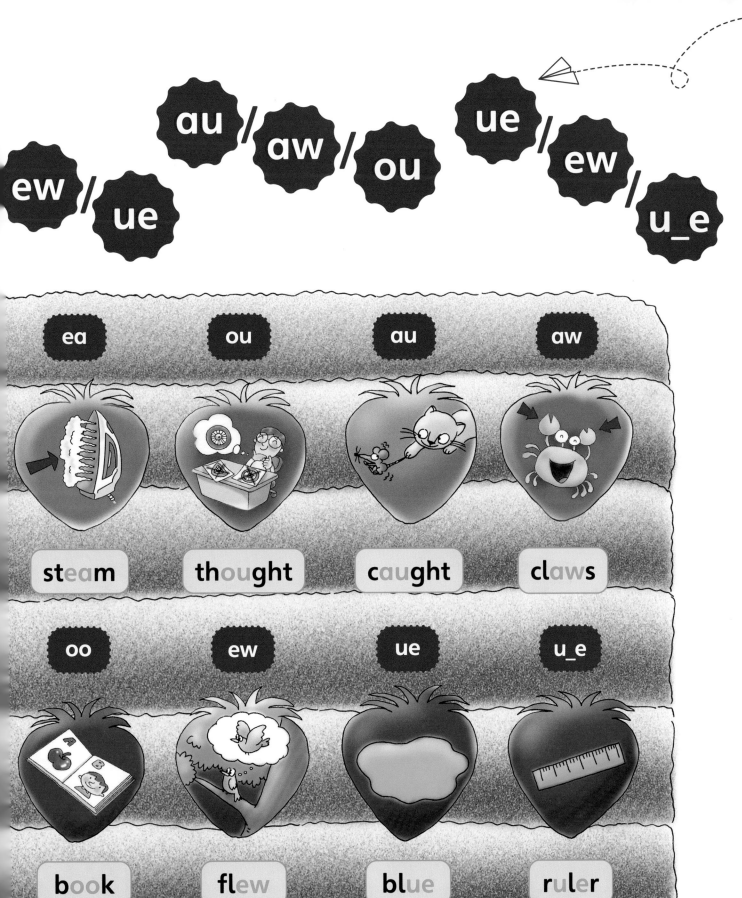

ew / ue

au / aw / ou

ue / ew / u_e

ea

ou

au

aw

steam

thought

caught

claws

oo

ew

ue

u_e

book

flew

blue

ruler

21

5 ur / or

ur

or

1

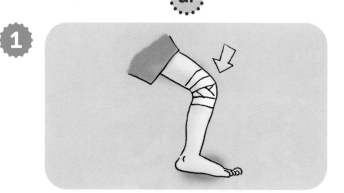

hurt

2

word

3

curtain

4

work

5

furry

6

worm

2   **Listen and read.**

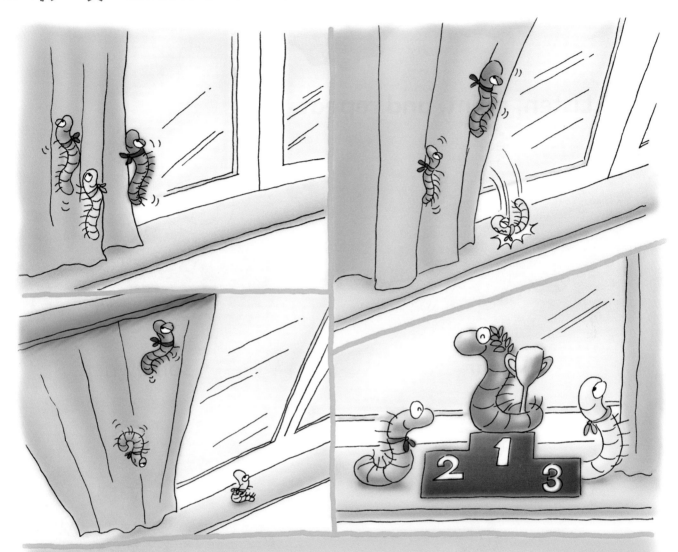

Three furry little worms climbing up the curtain,
One fell down and hurt himself.
Two furry little worms climbing up the curtain,
One turned back, it was such hard work.
One furry little worm climbing up the curtain,
He is the winning worm!

3 **Design a prize for the winning worm.**

5 **ear/ere**

4 **Listen, point, and repeat.**

ear

ere

1

b**ear**

2

somewh**ere**

3

t**ear**

4

th**ere**

5

w**ear**

6

wh**ere**

5  Listen. Then say.

Where, oh where, is my teddy bear?
I think I lost him over there.
He was wearing a new blue jacket,
which I hope he doesn't tear.
Where, oh where, is my teddy bear?

6 Can you find the teddy bear in the picture?

6  our / ower

1 Listen, point, and repeat.

our

ower

 1

h**our**

 4

fl**ower**

 2

our

 5

sh**ower**

 3

s**our**

 6

t**ower**

2  Listen. Then say.

The king lives in a big, tall tower.
He takes a shower every hour
and smells as sweet as a flower.

3 Write another tongue twister. How fast can you say it?

6 ire

4 🎧28 Listen, point, and repeat.

1

f**ire**

2

h**ire**

3

t**ire**

4

w**ire**

5

exp**ire**

6

adm**ire**

5  **Listen. Then say.**

🇺🇸 American	🇬🇧 British
fire truck	fire engine

Clang, clang, clang!
There goes the fire engine,
Rushing to put out the fires.
Zoom, zoom, zoom!
There goes the racing car,
With the fastest ever tires.

6 **Write a story about a fire truck or a racing car.**

Review 3

1 🎧 30 Play the game. Say words with the same sound or words for the pictures. Then listen and check.

ear / ere

our / ower

ire

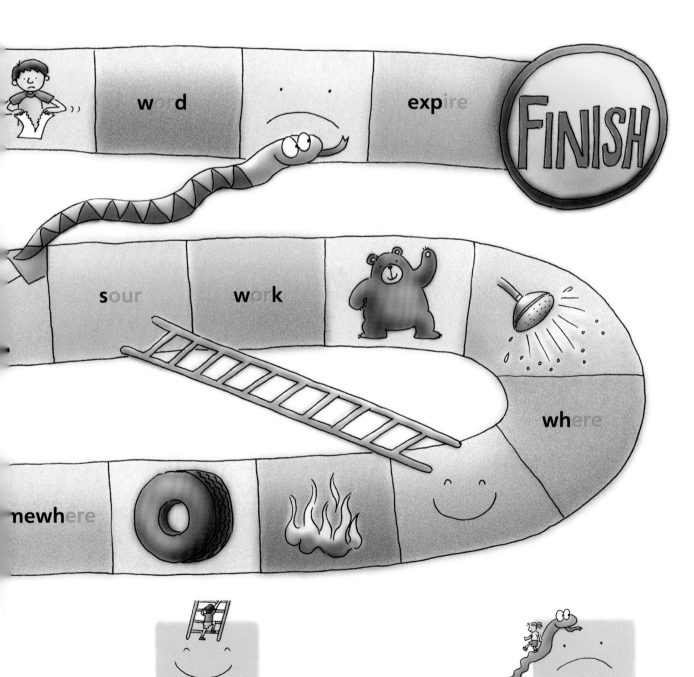

w**or**d

exp**ire**

FINISH

s**our**

w**or**k

wh**ere**

newh**ere**

Silent letters (1)

 American
neighbors

 British
neighbours

1 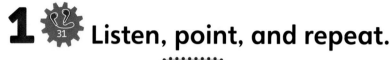 Listen, point, and repeat.

silent w

silent gh

 1

wrap

 4
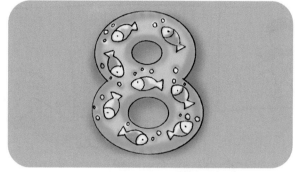
eight

2

wrinkles

5

naughty

 3

answer

6

neighbors

2  Listen. Then say.

I have ei**gh**t nau**gh**ty nei**gh**bors and they like to read and **w**rite.

They never get an answer **w**rong, they are always ri**gh**t.

They bou**gh**t some **w**rinkled paper to **w**rap a gift for a friend,

But they mi**gh**t forget to send it, even thou**gh** they are very bri**gh**t.

3  Draw a gift for a special friend.

7 Silent letters (2)

4 Listen, point, and repeat.

silent k

silent b

1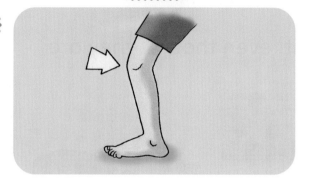

knee

4

climb

2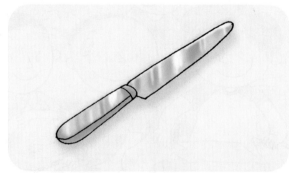

knife

5

lamb

3

knot

6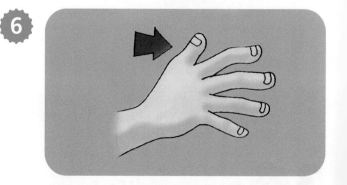

thumb

5 Listen and read.

We go camping in a tent.
We climb up a mountain.

Do you know how to tie a knot in a rope?
Can you cut the rope with a knife?
You must be careful.
Don't cut your knee or your thumb!

6 Act out the story.

Using *a & an* (1)

1 🎧 35 **Listen, point, and repeat.**

1

a **E**uropean

2
but

an **e**lephant

3
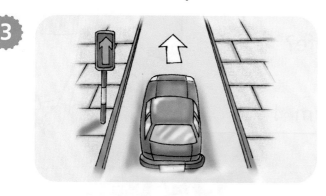
a **o**ne-way street

4
but

an **o**nion

5
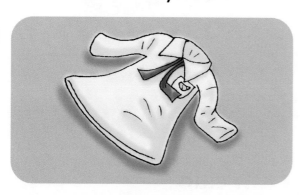
a **u**niform

6
but

an **u**ntidy room

2  **Listen and read.**

It's a wonderful thing to go to a youth club.
You may meet an elephant wearing a uniform
or a European eating an onion.
And best of all, you can forget that your mother
wants you to clean up an untidy room at home!

Concert

Computer

Painting

3  **What can you do in a youth club?**

4 🎧 37 Listen, point, and repeat.

1

a **h**oney bee

but

2

an **h**onest boy

3

a **m**an

but

4

an **M**TR station

5

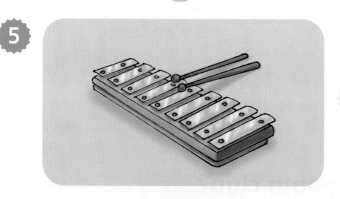

a **x**ylophone

but

6

an **X**-ray machine

5 🎵 **Listen. Then sing.**

Phonics fun, phonics fun,

Remember when we'd just begun?

Now we know it's *an* for an American but *a* for a European.

And it's just *a* for a man but *an* for an MTR station.

Phonics fun, phonics fun.

Congratulations on all you've done!

And don't forget,

Phonics is fun!

6 🌼 **Think of other examples with *a* and *an*.**
Write another song and sing it.

Review 4

1 🎧 **40 Play the game. Say the words and clap if there are silent letters. Say words for the pictures, using *a* or *an*. Then listen and check.**

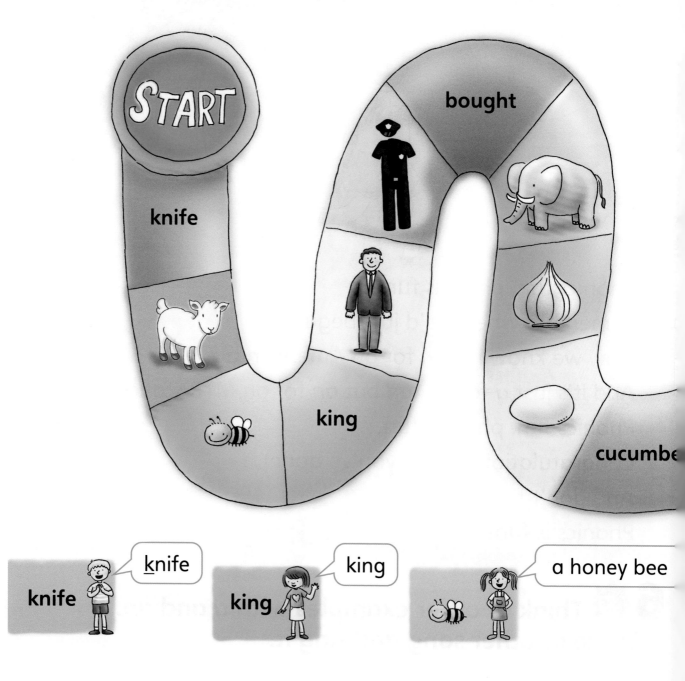

START

knife

bought

king

cucumbe

knife	<u>k</u>nife	
king	king	
	a honey bee	

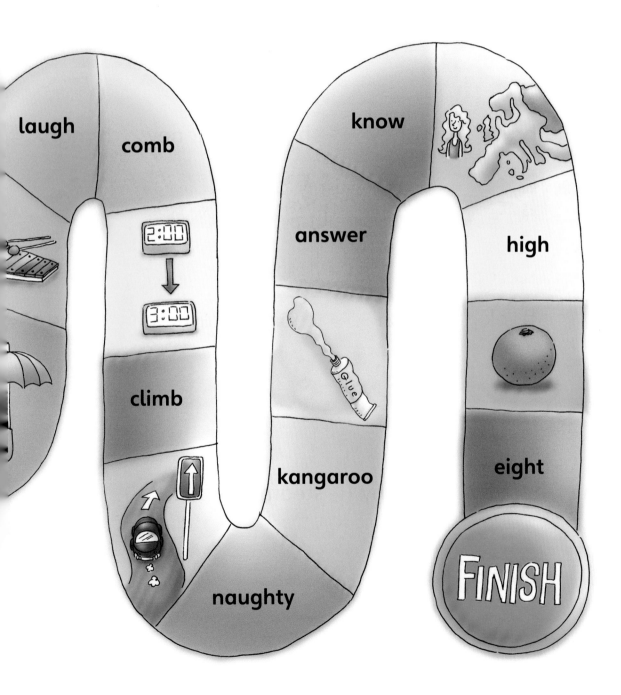

laugh

comb

climb

naughty

know

answer

kangaroo

high

eight

FINISH

PHONICS DICTIONARY

a o	wash	fog	what	hot	want	shop

o u	son	brush	honey	hug	money	hungry

u oo	put	book	push	cook	cushion	good

short ea long ea	headline	healthy	wealthy	steam	eat	sea

 oa
 ow

boat	blow	coat	flow	road	snow

 ew
 ue

view	few	interview	Sue	glue	clue

 au
 aw
ou

caught	August	saw	claws	bought	thought

 ue
 ew
 u_e

blue	true	drew	flew	June	ruler

PHONICS DICTIONARY

 ur
 or

hurt	word	curtain	work	furry	worm

 ear
 ere

bear	somewhere	tear	there	wear	where

 our
 ower

hour	flower	our	shower	sour	tower

ire

fire	hire	tire	wire	expire	admire

silent w	**w**rap	**w**rinkles	ans**w**er	ei**gh**t	nau**gh**ty	nei**gh**bors
silent gh						

silent k	**k**nee	**k**nife	**k**not	clim**b**	lam**b**	thum**b**
silent b						

	a **E**uropean	an **e**lephant	a **o**ne way street	an **o**nion	a **u**niform	an **u**ntidy room
a & an						

	a **h**oney bee	an **h**onest boy	a **m**an	an **M**TR station	a **x**ylophone	an **X**-ray machine
a & an						

Pearson Education Limited
KAO TWO
KAO Park
Hockham Way
Harlow, Essex
CM17 9SR
England
and Associated Companies throughout the world.

english.com/englishcode

Authorized Licenced Edition from the English language edition, entitled Phonics Fun, 1st edition
published Pearson Education Asia Limited, Hong Kong and Longman Asia ELT © 2003.

This Edition © Pearson Education Limited 2021

First published 2021
Third impression 2024
ISBN: 978-1-292-32266-7
Set in Heinemann Roman 17/19pt

Printed in Slovakia by Neografia

Illustrated by Christos Skaltsas (Hyphen S.A.)